# Golf For Beginners

*Learn How to Play Golf, the Rules of Golf, and Other Golf Tips for Beginners*

by Jim Stonich

# Table of Contents

# Introduction

As a wise golfer once said, "Golf is a game of four inches."

Most people take the "four inches" to be a reference to the diameter of the cup (the hole where the golf ball eventually ends up). But to the seasoned golfer, however, the referenced four inches have nothing to do with the cup and instead are referring to the four inches of space behind your eyes, the operational headquarters of the brain's frontal lobe.

Golf is unique in that it is a solitary sport. In competitive golf, another player's performance will have absolutely no effect on your performance and vice versa. In even the most elite of high-profile golf competitions, all golfers are ultimately competing against no one other than themselves. This is why it's important, as you learn and grow in the game, to play within your own capability. One of the most frequent and preventable mistakes that golfers make at every skill level is attempting to emulate or keep up with their peers. If you're just beginning to play, don't expect (or try) to become a golf pro overnight. Instead, just focus on accepting your game for what it is and gradually steering yourself towards excellence. Good golfing is patient golfing.

This book is designed to be a beginner's guide to the basics of golf. It won't turn you into Tiger Woods, but it will certainly prevent you from seeming clueless or having to ask embarrassing questions on the course. By the end of this book, you'll know what clubs to use, how to hold them, the rules of the game, how the scoring system works, and important golf etiquette. Let's get started!

# Chapter 1: Is Golf the World's Simplest Game?

Seems fairly straightforward right? Get the ball in the hole. Sure you need to understand which clubs to use and when, how to adjust for wind, and how to avoid the bunkers (sand traps), but that's about it, right?

Well, yes and no. Sure, the essentials of being successful at golf boil down to putting the ball in the hole with as few strokes as possible. But there are a myriad of other factors to consider, each one adding more layers of nuance to this ostensibly simple game:

- Shots you make on a golf course can be made at a variety of angles, including uphill, downhill, and sidehill. You also have uphill/sidehill and downhill/sidehill combination angles.

- Golf can be influenced by the weather.

- The grass used on golf courses can differ course to course. The type of grass and the way it's mowed can affect your shots.

- Golf course features such as coral, bridges, and embedded wooden bunkers may present unique challenges for the golfer

- Trees, wild grass, and rocks can disrupt shots anywhere on the golf course.

- Sand traps can be found anywhere on the golf course. Sand traps have different types of sand. They also vary significantly in their size and depth.

- Water features such as rivers, lakes, and ponds may pop up anywhere on the course and prove to be challenging obstacles.

- There's a multitude of golf clubs to learn about and choose from: four different types of woods, eight types of irons, as well as putters, sand wedges, and pitching wedges.

- Every course is different and every golf hole plays differently.

So no, when it comes to what you need to know to get started, Golf isn't hard. But an in depth look at the sport however will reveal that it is not without its subtleties.

In the next chapter we'll take a look at what beginning golfers can do to make sure they get off to a good start in the sport.

# Chapter 2: Golfing, Where to Begin

If you're just beginning, then you don't want to just grab some clubs, hop in a cart and beeline for the next open course. You're first going to need a bit of orientation and practice.

## Step 1: Time to Go Clubbing

You can't play golf without clubs, but you can certainly play golf without busting your bank trying to obtain the latest and greatest designer golf clubs right out of the gate. If you're just beginning to play, don't make a big investment in your clubs, but instead prepare yourself to focus on learning the game.

You don't need a lot of clubs when you're first beginning. Start with these:

**Driver-** The driver, also known as a 1 wood, is what you use to "tee-off" at the beginning of most medium to long-distance holes. The driver has the lowest "loft" of any club, save the putter. The "loft" is the angle of the face of the club that controls the trajectory of the shot. Low lofts are more perpendicular to the ground (like a putter, which has a 0 degree loft), while high lofts scoop upwards towards a more parallel alignment with the ground. The driver has a loft between 7 and 12 degrees. When selecting your driver, choose one with a higher loft, at least 10 degrees, as this will make it easier to make clean contact and sail the ball into the air.

**Putter-** The mission of the putter is to put your ball in the hole. Putters are used after you've successfully hit your ball onto the "green" – the green is the part of the hole that contains the pin (flagstick), where the grass is kept extra short so the ball rolls easily. While putters come in a variety of styles, they are usually flat faced (with a loft of zero degrees) perfectly perpendicular to the ground.

**Sand Wedge-** Also known as a sand-iron, this club has a loft of 54 to 56 degrees and is used for getting your ball out of sand traps. Because of its unique design, your Sand Wedge will often be your heaviest club.

**6 Iron-** This is the middle-of-the-road unit in your set of irons, which run from 2 to 9. The 6 iron is fairly easy to hit and can move the ball a little over a hundred yards.

**8 Iron-** The 8 Iron has a higher loft and is good for hitting high over trees or other obstacles. It is also useful for ensuring the ball lands "soft" on the green, meaning without much roll.

**Pitching Wedge-** This club will come in handy when you land your ball just outside of the green and need a short, controlled, "pitch shot" to get your ball onto the green and near the pin.

**Fairway Wood/Hybrid-** This club is used for power drives that don't begin on the tee-boxes (where you hit the ball at the beginning of the hole). You can use this club on the second or third shot of your hole and hit directly off the ground to get great distance. When selecting your first fairway wood, go with the one that has a 17 degree loft rather than a 15 degree loft. It will be easier to make clean contact with the ball.

Start with this simple set of clubs. Once you get comfortable using them, you will naturally progress to a greater variety of clubs.

With regard to buying your clubs, if you are just beginning, go to a larger golf store and ask to try two 6 Irons, one with a regular flex shaft and another with a stiff flex shaft. The faster and more aggressive your swing, the more likely you'll feel more comfortable with the shaft labeled "s" for stiff. Choose the shaft that feels easiest to control.

Also, be sure to ask about clubs that are tailored specifically for beginners. These clubs can often be identified as having wider than normal soles (the very bottom part of the club where its number is usually inscribed).

## *Step 2: Getting the Right Type and Amount of Balls*

Golf balls are often referred to as coming in "sleeves," which is slang for a group of three balls. If you are just beginning, you should count on losing a fair amount of golf balls. Buy balls that cost about $20 for a dozen and have at least a dozen available to you for 9 holes. If you're having trouble picking one brand over another, try hitting a few on the practice green to get a better feel for your purchase.

## *Step 3: Get Ready to Learn*

It's helpful to know from the beginning whether you're pursuing golf as a fun way to pass time with friends every now and again, or whether you'd like to develop highly sound and competitive skills in the sport. Knowing your intentions for the game will help you make important choices like whether to join a club and whom to seek out for instruction.

Generally, it's a good idea to get help right out of the gate. Sign up for some lessons. If you're serious about becoming a good golfer, seek out the instruction of a

14

PGA professional. Regardless of the experience level of your teacher, it's important to find someone with whom you have great chemistry. You need to be comfortable asking your instructor anything about the game. You need your instructor to be as serious minded (or as laid back) as you are about developing your golf game.

## Step 4: How to Be at Home on the Range

A lot of beginning players make the mistake of setting foot on the driving range and immediately seeing how far they can hit the ball. Don't do this. Use the driving range to warm up your "golf muscles" slowly. Start by hitting your pitching wedge or a short iron (2 - 4 iron) and gradually work your way up to your middle irons and woods. After you work your way up, work your way back down again. This will help you regulate your tempo and tension.

## Step 5: Drill the Short Game

Practicing your short game may not be as glamorous as cranking out drives, but it is a necessity if you want to be a good golfer. Approximately half of your shots you make during your golfing career will occur within 50 yards of the green, so you've got to practice your chip and putt as much as you can.

The good news is that you can do this in the comfort of your own home, at least the putting. Practice putting through furniture legs and through doorways. Get one of those portable golf hole contraptions with the automatic ball return and keep it handy in your office. As for practicing your chips and pitches aka approach shots, you can do this in your backyard or at the golf club in the designated area.

# Chapter 3: Calling the Shots

Before you set foot on your first 9 hole run, you need to have some basic level of competency when it comes to understanding and making shots. You need to be able to tee up a ball and drive it along the fairway. It need not be a drive of galactic caliber, but you should be able to get the ball up into the air and sailing generally in the right direction. You will also need to be able to connect on the fairway or in the rough with an iron or fairway wood and advance your ball further towards the green.

## The Grip

Grip your golf club with your dominant hand placed lower on the club handle than your non-dominant hand. Sometimes it helps to interlock the pinky on your leading/dominant hand with the forefinger of your other hand. Choke up or down on the club enough to enable a smooth swing through the playable space near the ground.

## The Drive

Though the driver is the largest club in the bunch, it is not necessarily the most difficult to swing. Don't be intimidated by it. Start by teeing the ball up nice and high. When you hit the ball with the driver, imagine that the ball is not there at all. Swing *through* the ball. Remember, though golf is an extremely mental sport, the act of swinging, especially during the drive, is an athletic act. Stronger players are going to swing harder. More coordinated players are going to make better and more frequent contact. When you finish the shot, hold your finish. The ability to which you can hold your finish smoothly is a good gage of whether or not you're swinging at a speed you can control.

## Chips and Pitches

One important shot distinction is that between a pitch and a chip. A pitch involves a high arc for the ball in the air where you attempt to land the ball "soft," close to the pin with minimal rolling after the ball hits the ground. A pitch shot uses a much shallower arc and is intended to make the ball roll further towards the pin after it lands.

## The Greenside Bunker

The greenside bunker shot is a shot where the head of the club actually makes no contact with the ball. Instead, you strike the sand just behind the ball and the force from the sand pushes the ball up into the air and out of the bunker. This means that your swing is going to be a bit stronger than your standard swing strength.

To hit a greenside bunker, align the instep of your leading foot with the ball. Position your feet slightly inwards for stability (you are standing on sand after all). Swing back about halfway then strike the sand about two inches behind the ball, turning your torso smoothly forward as you swing to finish your shot facing the direction of the target.

## *Putting*

Not much can be said about the putt other than keep your eye on the ball, swing and follow through, and be aware of the gradients of the putting green. Most importantly, practice makes perfect. A good putting game can be a powerful asset to your overall golf prowess.

# Chapter 4: The Right Course

Are you shored up on all your fundamentals and ready for a real golf course? Great. If golf was the corporate world, then beginning golfers would go straight to the top by playing "Executive Courses." Executive courses are composed of predominantly par 3 holes, meaning that the target stroke count to complete each hole is 3 strokes. These are shorter holes, usually less than 200 yards. They may contain a few par 4 and par 5 holes, but even these are significantly shorter on executive courses.

It's crucial for golfers to sustain their focus and confidence during their game, remember golf is a game of 4 inches. Your endurance as a golfer needs to be developed just like the other attributes of your game. For this reason, you should start by playing just three holes, while striving to maintain your best possible focus and skill level. A good practice is to try and find courses or times of day that are less in-demand so you can proceed with minimal interruption and distraction. If you're unable to find a course that allows you to pay for just three holes at a time, then go ahead and pay for a 9 hole game, but don't push yourself to play on if you're getting frustrated or mentally tired. Go back to the driving range or practice greens and regroup.

When you select a course, be sure to play from the front-most tee boxes. You will usually see two to four tee boxes of different color on any given hole. They are there to allow you some extra distance on your game, so take advantage of them. Also, choose a course that is more basic and straightforward for your first several golf outings. Try to avoid courses that have a great deal of obstacles that will prevent you from reaching the fairway or interrupt your progress to the hole.

If you're having a tough time on a hole there's no shame in picking up your ball after the $7^{th}$ or $8^{th}$ stroke. Doing this will help keep the pace of your game where it belongs. A good recommendation for pacing is four and a half hours for eighteen holes. Maintaining proper pacing during your golfing is an important component of golf etiquette, which we'll talk more about in the following chapter.

# Chapter 5: Prim and Proper

The sport of golf has a strong connotation with luxury, affluence, and propriety. It's an annoying but inescapable part of the sport and the culture that surrounds it. As is true with so much in life, even if you don't intend on perfectly abiding by all the rules, it's good to *know* the rules *before* you break them.

One rule you should never ever break is calling out "fore" when there is even a remote chance of a golf ball hitting another player. Don't hesitate or wait to see which direction the wind blows the suspect ball, just yell. And be sure to yell loud enough to be heard. It's also helpful to give directions when you yell "fore" like "fore right" or "fore left."

Golf carts should never be on the green or even near the green. In fact, some courses prefer that golf carts never leave the cart path. Be sure to check with the court you're playing on to see what the norms are for cart usage.

Take care of the course you're playing on. If you make divots in the court with a bad swing, then do your best to repair the hole by refilling it and patting it down with your foot. If you have to hit a shot out of a sand bunker, then be sure to rake the bunker after you finish so other players will have as even as possible surface to hit from should their ball find similar fates.

Don't talk when waiting for a player to hit their swing and stand behind them and *to the right* (if the player is a right-handed player). You never know when mental fatigue will have its day and a golf club goes hurling behind someone's back left.

When your opponents are putting, try to avoid being in their line of site and never walk through the area between their ball and the cup.

Regarding order of play, usually the player who had the lowest score on the previous hole has "the honor" and hits first. After everyone has taken their initial swing, play proceeds with the player whose ball is furthest away from the hole. The first player to reach the green in close proximity to the pin (the flag), is responsible for removing the flag for any player who no longer needs the flag to see the cup. Once the entire group has played the hole, the flag tender must be sure to replace the flag so the following party can see their target.

A good rule of thumb is to always remain at least a half hole behind the group playing in front of you. That said, you don't want to lag behind and slow the pace of your game. When it's your turn, take a few practice swings and hit your ball. Even with an upbeat steadily moving tempo, there will still be plenty of time to hang out and talk, broker deals, and guzzle whiskey.

# Chapter 6: The Language of the Golf Score

Even as a beginner, you should know the basic language of scoring in golf.

Every hole on a golf course is assigned a number that is the hole's "par." This is the number of strokes that an average player would need to complete the hole. "Par" is the measuring point for golf scoring, all other scoring terminologies are derived based on their relation to par. For instance, a "bogey" occurs when a player requires one more stroke than par. A "birdie" is achieved when a player requires one less stroke than par. Finishing a hole two strokes over par is known as a "double bogey" and two strokes under par is known as an "eagle."

Scoring for a round of golf is amazingly simple: the lowest score wins.

# Chapter 7: More Rules

A lot of golfers just make things up as they go. There are in fact 34 formal rules for golf, but all you really need to know are the following:

Don't touch your ball. The only time you should touch your ball with your hands is if it lands on the putting green and another player needs it moved so they can have a clear path to the pin OR if you find your ball trapped behind an obstruction, like a yardage marker or a fuse box or some other manmade item that was not intended to be an obstacle for the golf course. If you need to move your ball on the putting green, use a coin or a plastic ball marker disc to hold the position of your ball.

If you hit your ball out of bounds (outside of a course's white out of bounds markers), then take a one stroke penalty and take another shot from the same location.

Don't spend more than five minutes looking for a ball in the rough (the area beyond the fairway, often wooded or with taller grass. If you can't locate your ball after five minutes, take a one stroke penalty and retry your shot from the same location (the location where you were when you hit the ball into the rough). If you're not sure exactly where you were, make the best possible guess. Go to that area hold out your arm and drop the ball and play it from where it lands.

# Conclusion

Golf can be a whole lot of fun, especially for people who enjoy being outdoors in beautiful landscapes and who enjoy a mental challenge. Despite its reputation, there really isn't an enormous financial barrier to getting involved with golf. Many cities have public courses that are exceptionally reasonable, and as was mentioned earlier in this book, it's actually *not* a good idea to load up on a bunch of high-end golf clubs right out of the gate. Get some good beginner equipment and start off light and simple.

Golf is not only a game of patience and concentration, but it's also one of self-realization. At all levels of play, you must strive to leverage what you can do and accept what you can't do. In golf, no matter how illustrious your competition, you are always playing primarily against one person, yourself. Master your fear of your own shadow, and you'll be well on your way to becoming a fabulous golfer.

Finally, I'd like to thank you for purchasing this book! If you enjoyed it or found it helpful, I'd greatly appreciate it if you'd take a moment to leave a review on Amazon. Thank you!

Printed in Great Britain
by Amazon

45504078R00030